JUNIOR BIOGRAPHIES

Heather Moore Niver

CHANCE THE RAPPER

HIP-HOP ARTIST

Enslow Publishing
101 W. 23rd Street
Suite 240
New York, NY 10011
USA
enslow.com

WORDS TO KNOW

contract An agreement between an artist and record company to make and sell an album.

gospel A type of Christian music.

industry A business.

marijuana A plant that can be made into a drug to be smoked.

mixtape A collection of songs that is not released through a record company.

open mic A time in a club when people can perform, often music, comedy, or poetry.

positivity A good attitude or feeling.

producer The person who takes care of making a musical recording.

rap A kind of music in which words are spoken in rhythm or with speed.

record label A record company.

unsigned Not having a contract.

CONTENTS

Chance the Rapper

CHAPTER 1

CHANCE'S CHILDHOOD

Chancelor Johnathan Bennett is better known as Chance the Rapper these days. He was born on April 16, 1993, in Chicago, Illinois. His father, Ken, worked for the government. At one time, he worked for former president Barack Obama when Obama was a senator. He also worked for the city of Chicago. Lisa, his mother, works for the Illinois attorney general. Chance's little brother, Taylor, is also a rapper.

YOUNG MUSICIAN

Young Chancelor loved all kinds of music. "I've known I wanted to rap since I was in grade school," he says. At Jones College Prep High School, he and a friend started a hip-hop duo called Instrumentality. As a teenager, Chancelor started joining open-mic and poetry nights.

Chance Says:

"I guess [my confidence] is mostly from my dad, who taught me to stand for something, to have integrity and a set of ideals."

Chance's family has been an important part of his success. Here he poses with his mother, Lisa, in 2017.

He performed in front of a crowd of hundreds. Chancelor knew he could make a positive difference in the world through music. Soon he recorded his mixtapes *Good Enough* and *The Back to School Pack EP*.

A TURNING POINT

During high school, Chancelor became discouraged. His teachers didn't support his musical goals. He began running around with kids who took a lot of drugs. In 2012, Chancelor was suspended for having marijuana at school. While he was stuck at home, Chancelor began recording his first full-length mixtape: *10 Day* (also called *#10Day*).

Two months later, Chancelor was making waves in the music and rap industry. *Complex* magazine listed him as one of "10 New Chicago Rappers to Watch Out For." He was only eighteen years old. He had become Chance the Rapper.

Chance the Rapper sometimes calls himself Chano when he raps.

CHAPTER 2
CHANGES AND CHOICES

In 2013, Chance the Rapper announced that he would perform a 500-seat show in Chicago. It sold out! Soon he had the chance to tour with rapper and singer Childish Gambino. This helped him decide he wasn't in a hurry to sign with a record label. He liked to do things his own way.

Chance was working on a new mixtape called *Acid Rap*. He quickly realized he had everything he needed to produce it without a label. So he made his album and made it available online—for free. When he was on tour with rapper and producer Mac Miller, Chance saw that the kids in the audience knew all the words to his songs.

Chance Says:

"It's not about the music being free. It's about how it is displayed and made accessible and about artistic power. It was always about the artist-to-fan relationship."

Chance the Rapper performs at a 2013 concert in Cleveland, Ohio.

ON HIS OWN

Acid Rap made the *Billboard* chart, which lists the most popular albums. And it got the attention of major record labels. Chance began shopping around for a good record deal. He was ready to sign a contract with someone. But Chance turned all the offers down. He was making money without the support of a big music company.

Chance the Rapper is interviewed by TV host and rapper Bow-Wow.

Chance the Rapper performed on *Saturday Night Live* in December 2015. He was the show's first unsigned musical guest.

CHOICES

By now, Chance had a serious drug problem. His family told him to get his act together. Chance didn't listen at first. But then he watched as one of his friends was killed. This was a wake-up call. He and his dad had a serious talk about Chance's future. After that, his dad started to handle his music career.

Chance attends a Chicago Bulls basketball game with his girlfriend, Kirsten Corley.

In the next six months, Chance quit doing drugs. He felt called to religion. Then he and his girlfriend, Kirsten, got some exciting news. Kirsten was pregnant. Chance the Rapper was going to be Chance the father, too.

Chance and his girlfriend were excited about becoming parents. Then they got some scary news. Their baby's heart did not beat the way it should. Terrified, Chance prayed. Baby Kinsley Bennett was born on September 21, 2015. She was healthy. Chance thanked God for answering his prayers.

A NEW STYLE

Chance was ready to work on a new album. He spent two months feverishly working on his project. This mixtape

Chance the Rapper wrote the foreword to the 2017 book *A People's History of Chicago* by Kevin Coval.

Chance the Rapper accepts the Grammy for Best New Artist in 2017.

was a totally new style for him. *Coloring Book*'s topics included love, dance, and Chicago. It also referred to Bible verses and included a song called "Blessings." On February 12, 2017, he made history. Chance, the unsigned, independent artist won three Grammy Awards.

CHANCE TALKS CHRISTIANITY

Finding his faith was a huge change for Chance. He doesn't go to church every Sunday, but Chance is outspoken about his faith. When he won his Grammy Awards, he accepted them by saying, "Glory be to God,

Chance Says:

"I love my family. I love God. And I love music."

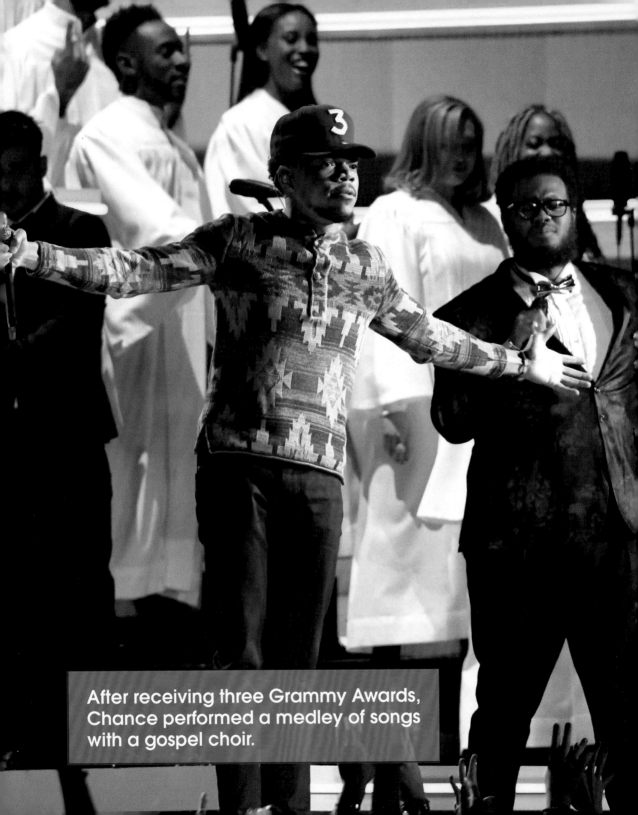

After receiving three Grammy Awards, Chance performed a medley of songs with a gospel choir.

I claim the victory in the name of the Lord! … I claim the victory in the name of Jesus Christ!" Then he sang with a choir and two gospel musicians.

Chance does not worry too much about labels, like what kind of Christian he is. "I just know what I'm supposed to do and what I'm not supposed to do, you know?"

CHAPTER 4
THE CHARITY OF CHANCE

Chance loves Chicago. He helped to build an organization called SocialWorks. It hosts events that encourage positivity in the community. One event was 2016's Parade to the Polls. Chance led thousands of young people in a march to the election polls and also gave them a free concert!

In March 2017, Chance made a huge donation to support Chicago public schools. He also personally donated another $10,000 for every $100,000 raised by

In August 2017, Chance headed out to the barbeque grills to raise money for Chicago public schools.

SocialWorks for Chicago's public schools. Twenty schools received more than $2 million in donations!

Chance reaches out to the students, too. In August 2017, Chance was the grand marshal of a parade for kids. To get them excited about going back to school, Chance arranged for 30,000 backpacks to be passed out. The packs were stuffed with school supplies.

WARMEST WINTER 2016

Winters in Chicago can be freezing cold! Chance worked with the Empowerment Plan to get special jackets to the

Chance continues to give back to his hometown of Chicago. In 2017, he donated $1 million to Chicago public schools.

Chance spends time taking selfies with fans in Chicago.

homeless. EMPWR jackets are waterproof and warm. They also turn into sleeping bags. The coats were made in Detroit, Michigan. This offered training and jobs to people living in nearby homeless shelters.

Chance Says:

"Depending on the story that you're telling, you can be relatable to everybody or nobody. I try and tell everybody's story."

SIGNED, AT LAST!

In 2017, Chance hired American Sign Language interpreters called DEAFinitely Dope. They joined his *Coloring Book* tour. He wanted everyone, including the deaf, to enjoy the show. His video announcement included an interpreter signing with him.

Who knows what Chance the Rapper will be up to next. But it's sure to be interesting, creative, and generous!

Chance the Rapper in concert in 2017

TIMELINE

1993 Chancelor Johnathan Bennett is born on April 16 in Chicago, Illinois.

2012 Chance the Rapper releases his first album, *10 Day.*

2013 *Acid Rap* is released.

2015 Chance performs on his brother Taylor's album, *Broad Shoulders.*

Daughter Kinsley Bennett is born on September 21.

Becomes the first unsigned musical guest to perform on *Saturday Night Live.*

2016 Releases his third mixtape, *Coloring Book.* It becomes the first-ever streaming-only album to rise to the top of the *Billboard* 200. It hit number 8!

Wins his first three Grammy Awards for Best New Artist, Best Rap Performance, and Best Rap Album.

2017 Makes *Time* magazine's "100 Most Influential People" list.

Wins the BET Humanitarian of the Year Award for his charity and donations.

BOOKS

Hill, Laban Carrick, and Theodore Taylor III. *When the Beat Was Born: DJ Kool Herc and the Creation of Hip Hop.* New York, NY: Roaring Brook Press, 2013.

Royston, Angela. *Hip-Hop.* Chicago, IL: Raintree, 2014.

Sacks, Nathan. *American Hip-Hop: Rappers, DJs, and Hard Beats.* Minneapolis, MN: Lerner Publishing Group, 2017.

WEBSITES

Chance the Rapper

chanceraps.com

Check out videos, photos, events, and more at Chance the Rapper's official website.

How to Rap

johnfosterchildrenspoet.co.uk/index.php/getting-started/21-rap/25
Learn how to spin your own spoken poetry or raps.

SocialWorks

socialworkschi.org

Learn about the events and causes this organization hosts and supports.

INDEX

Published in 2019 by Enslow Publishing, LLC.
101 W. 23rd Street, Suite 240, New York, NY 10011

Library of Congress Cataloging-in-Publication Data
Names: Niver, Heather Moore, author.
Title: Chance the Rapper : hip-hop artist / Heather Moore Niver.
Description: New York, NY : Enslow Publishing, 2019. | Series: Junior biographies | Includes bibliographical references and index. | Audience: Grades 3-6.
Identifiers: LCCN 2017046602| ISBN 9780766097155 (library bound) | ISBN 9780766097162 (pbk.) | ISBN 9780766097179 (6 pack)
Subjects: LCSH: Chance the Rapper Juvenile literature, | Rap musicians–United States–Biography–Juvenile literature.
Classification: LCC ML3930.C442 N58 2019 | DDC 782.421649092 [B] –dc23
LC record available at https://lccn.loc.gov/2017046602

Printed in the United States of America

To Our Readers: We have done our best to make sure all website addresses in this book were active and appropriate when we went to press. However, the author and the publisher have no control over and assume no liability for the material available on those websites or on any websites they may link to. Any comments or suggestions can be sent by e-mail to customerservice@enslow.com.